SONG
OF THE
MOUNTAINS

Song of the Mountains

© 2023, John C. Mannone

Books may be purchased in quantity and/or special sales by contacting the publisher. All inquiries related to such matters should be addressed to:

Middle Creek Publishing & Audio
9161 Pueblo Mountain Park Road
Beulah, CO 81023
editor@middlecreekpublishing.com
(719) 369-9050

First Paperback Edition, 2023
ISBN:978-1-957483-16-0
Cover Design: David Anthony Martin

SONG
OF THE
MOUNTAINS

John C. Mannone

Middle Creek Publishing & Audio
Beulah, CO USA

Introduction

Song of the Mountains is a poetic celebration, eulogy, and metaphor for Appalachia. Sometimes it dances and laughs, but too many times it cries. It's a vehicle to give voice to creation, a prayer, psalm or hymn of nature. It's an echo of the past merging with the present. The mountains speak in these songs, the culture of Appalachia—food, family, religion & spirituality, a place of dreams, politics, ecology, and mining, but a place of loss, too, both of its people and their land—the desecration of that land, which is like cursing God. Place is as sacred as family. Depression, a byproduct, runs deep, as a vein of ore in a coal mine. Yet the heart is sometimes blacker than coal searching for the silver and gold threading it like false promises do. Sometimes there are no clear differences. For all the good and evil in our hearts, we love as deeply as we mourn, and that music of the mountains is a salve, as well as a song.

Table of Contents

To all my fellow Appalachians, whose music pierced my heart. It wasn't just the banjo and guitar, the fiddle and the base, but also their voices lifted from their heartaches for the mountains...

and to the mountains themselves whose lament I hear as I write.

Opening

Come Swing on the Porch With Me
and I'll Kindle Your Heart

I am great
smoky mountain air
older than rocky
mountain stone. I am lifted-up
sandstone, soft
jazzy grasslands.

I am green-water
the sky shed as tears,
my lifeblood flowing
through the great valley
wandering to the Mississippi,
lapping at sycamores; I leave
you river pearls.

I am tulip poplar,
the mockingbird's song
nesting in flowering
dogwood, and redbud
when spring does to me what
I want to do to you. I am wild
iris, your passion
flower, I am a tiger
lily for honeybees
and zebra swallowtails.

I am intoxicating moon
shine, delirious
in honeysuckle sun
calling your name.

Part 1

Carrots

My grandfather's fingers shook a little
until they clamped the base of the plant
as if ready to yank weeds. Gently,
he coaxed the root to the surface—
the bulbous end cresting loamy clay.
Muted orange poked through the soil
as if a morning sun lifting through mist.
Dirt clung to the carrot. He rubbed it
off leaving that good scent of earth
on his hands. He snapped the green leaf
canopy clear off, let it drop to the ground,
and dangled the tapered end in front
of my face. The tendrils whiskering
the carrot caught the same glints
as grandpa's white hairs stubbling his chin.
He urged me to take a bite, to feel
the cool crisp flesh of carrot on my tongue,
taste its earthy sweetness.

I was barely six. His blue eyes winked
with wisdom. He said carrots were good
for my eyes, that they would help me see
more clearly the world outside this garden.

The Crack in the Cookie Jar

In my mother's kitchen, sunlight filtered through the window after sifting through a canopy of green leaves. A Tennessee Mountain Fig Tree planted by the creek. I was only four and I snuck in to find my favorite fruit—those figs that momma usually hid from me. I would hide behind the counter making sure that no one could see me except perhaps the shadows slipping on the floor, or on the cupboard doors. They moved like the wind; their dark edges grazed my eyes.

Soon I'd forget my fear and climb into the darkened recesses on top of the counter. A darker shadow lurked behind the white enameled door. I swung it open and light fell on a giant apple-shaped cookie jar; its yellow skin glowed, blushed with ripened reds and dainty'd with perfectly shaped green leaves from a ceramic tree. I could almost eat it.

I knelt on the countertop and reached for it with my right hand quivering. My tiny fingers stretched to hook the handle and pull the jar closer to me. A hollow sound echoed in the cabinet more empty than my memory, but my thoughts were heavy enough for me to know joy.

I shimmied to the floor before opening the jar. The ceramic top slid slowly, scraping like a coffin lid—the high-pitched sound of ghosts leaked out. I worked the jar closer to the sunlight and peered inside expecting to find a stash-pile of figs. There were none, not even the skeleton of one. But half in shadow, a single piece of fig cake edged into the light. I snatched it, which uncovered a crack in the cream white bottom of the cookie jar. I stared at it as I let the crumbs fall from my mouth, and felt a twitch of guilt.

~~~

Today, every time I see a cookie jar that's big and round, I look inside hoping for a fig, while imagining my mother's spirit sifting-in from the past through a crack in the ceramic. And that all my guilt would be gone. Instead, there's only the dark etch of a web—spider cracks of memory.

Bread & Butter Pickles

Flour-dusted bowls on the kitchen counter
testify to the work of bread. Warm yeast
blending with the still warm air seeped

into my memory. Wedged in the corner, the quiet
dash churn leaned its tall narrow cylinder of wood
with vestiges of butter-cream on the oaken plunger.

I remember the coriander floating with the cucumber
discs brined with turmeric, mustard and celery seeds.
Their yellow flesh splayed on buttered bread,

the honey-sweet taste hiding with vinegar
lingering in the Dust Bowl, well into the War.

Mom served those pickles after school
on bright porcelain dishes
fished out of *Duz* detergent boxes —

the small ones, with 24-carat gold rims
and amber wheat sheaves clustering their centers.

She carefully placed those plates on grandma's linen
that laced the middle of a thick-legged mahogany table,
its heavy, sculpted feet firm on the hardwood floor.

My sister and I dangled our legs from cushioned
chairs. We watched the afternoon sun glisten
on each other's faces, eyes as big as those

green-rimmed pickles; felt the cool crunch
between the warm slices of soft bread.

We never went hungry.

Shiitake Mushrooms

How to grow and eat them

After the river breeze dissolves
the morning fog, lay the axe wedge
a couple feet above the stump,
first, on the side of the felling,
      then behind, to let gravity
      pull and have its bending moment
      topple the tall tree to the ground.
      Saw-blade the fallen five-inch oak
tree into four-foot-long sections,
Drill inch-deep holes, a half-inch wide
—stagger in a diamond pattern.
Fill the holes with mycelia-
      -inoculated sawdust, then
      compact the holes before sealing
      with melted cheese wax by mopping
      with steady, patient paintbrush strokes.
Stack logs, crisscrossed, under the shade
of a stand of trees near the lake
where the logs can be dunked in case
the season is unusually dry.
      A year later, the harvesting
      of the fruit, the mushrooms themselves
      pop out of the colonized logs,
      their tan to burnt orange caps, shagged.

~~~

Slice and sauté them in butter,
thin-sliced shallots, thyme, and white wine.
A garlic-pine aroma, rich
with earth, releases an intense
      mythical power with the taste:
      soft, fleshy, yet chewy texture—
      buttery smoke, woodsy mushrooms
      full of dense umami flavor
[from the savory glutamates;
addictive neurochemicals
along with hallucinogens—

psilocybin and psilocin].
Perhaps well-suited to Let's Eat
Grandma, a psychedelic sludge
band: a couple of teenage girls
playing smeary, woozy, jazz-pop
breaking into a fitting rap
they call *Eat Shiitake Mushrooms*.

Mountain Food

Cited in 'A Mess of Greens: Southern Gender & Southern Food' by Elizabeth E. D. Englehardt:

[M]ountain men and women…were thought of, by tourists passing swiftly through the hills, as all of a type…dangerous, secretive, sly…[who] spent their time hunting 'federals' or shooting at each other…of course, all nonsense. They were of every type, incipient poets, hard-working men, killers, horse traders, liars, men faithful to friends unto death, stupid ones, smart ones, God-seeking ones.
—Sherwood Anderson, *Kit Brandon: A Portrait*

Who doesn't love hot, long-buttered
biscuits right out of the coal-fired pot
belly stove slathered with sorghum—
molasses-sharp to the tongue, or fresh
churned butter with a glass of buttermilk,

or baked bread made from soft-wheat
ground by the grist mill—its water wheel
dipping into the stream so clean that one
could pick watercress for sandwiches
in the fields, eat with hickory smoked ham,
cured in the cabin,

or skillet-fry mountain farm chickens
in a Dutch oven pan with a lid dappled
with raised metal nipples to collect steam
and oil before it rains a sizzle to braise,
tenderize in leaf lard or peanut oil before
lifting the lid to brown a delicious crust?

Some farming techniques came from
the Cherokees, like growing beans and squash
up corn stalks—corn itself a major staple
for cornbread and grits. Pawpaws, squirrel,
pike, and morels are common. Chores, endless
but shared among family and neighbors, and
celebrated with special desserts—black walnut-
coconut pound cake or blackberry cobbler.

Mountain food is more than food, eating
and storytelling around the dinner table
was always good in all of Appalachia.
The preservation of culture—one stereotype
that should survive.

Ohio writer, Sherwood Anderson (1876-1941) writes about the common folk
of Appalachia through the eyes of a poor hill country girl, Kit Brandon.

Collecting Stones with my Granddaughter

Big Frog Mountain overlooks the lillypad lake
where we'd swim. Near water's edge, she'd rake
the Indian Boundary sand; that cornmeal sand
floured through her small fingers as she sifted
for stones: flat ones that changed from dull gray
to smoky blue, and shined under water. She'd pluck
them out, they covered the palm of her hand as if
they were huge sweet raisins, then she'd run to her
lime-green bucket full of water and *kerplunk* them
along with the other silvery pieces of shale with a
salmon pink glitter.

But the real prizes were the lead-heavy chunks
shaped like cubes, some no wider than a pinky's
fingernail. Others too big to grapple with toes—
those were the gold. Their iron-black faces
of chalcopyrite glinted with a bit of copper. Akin
to fools' gold, but there were no fools on the beach
that day. Just a couple of folks on either end
of life. I'd bring her here so many times, yet
smiles of discovery were never lost, always fresh.
And when she'd bring me a busted stone, I'd stash
the memory in a pocket full of gold.

There was nothing
broken
in her little hands.

Working the Puzzle

Start with the pieces laid out
               in one layer
         Scan them for the straight edges
                       where borders hide
        among the dense forest
of jigsaw'd pulpwood paper
            Study the image on the box cover
               Get a sense of color
                   of object—blue sky, green leaves,
      purple water, dark brown
           mountains…Each one
a piece of cardboard painted
        with life
Scenes interlock   their empty spaces
        filling each other
        like an empty bay
           becoming water
There is always a sense
           of completion
        whenever there is a fit
           I always wanted to fit
      in with the rest of the crowd   even though
        they were broken as much as I—I could never see
the forest from the trees
        the ocean from the waves
           your smiles from the frowns
the white space from the gray

When the frame is outlined—daisy chained—pieces
inside link with a sense of focus and purpose
So I start the mosaic: dark with dark
                       Light with light

Blood

There's always some kind of war around these parts, as if Lyndon B. Johnson's declaration of *War on Poverty* wasn't enough; American involvement in Vietnam was rapidly escalating about the same time.

I was born a baby boomer in a tiny four-room shanty, newspaper crammed into the seams of pine board walls to stay the chill; the tin roof, a rusty scab. Daddy and Uncle Ronnie worked double shifts just so we could eat; coal dust always in the air. After the accident, Mama swore she wouldn't let me work in the mine. I was almost five and didn't understand why Daddy was gone. When the blood red moon poured its light over the winter pines, I cried out loud to the man up there like Daddy did so many times. Mama overheard and came running, grabbed hold of me and clutched me to her bosom, saying in a soft voice but straining not to crack, "It's okay, John David. *Shsh, shsh, shsh.* It's okay." She was crying, too. When I was older, Mama told me about the brakes of a dang coal truck that broke. Daddy didn't see or hear it coming in time to move before the runaway truck crushed him against the rock wall.

Mama said that for me to be successful, I would have to break the cycle: leave this place and go make something of myself. If I stayed, I'd probably be stuck here forever, probably die in some down-deep godforsaken mineshaft. But at least I wouldn't miss the cherry-fizz phosphates with my sweetheart, Becky Ann, at the corner Five & Dime. But how does someone poorer than dirt-poor get to go to college?

When that other war broke out, the one in Southeast Asia that I didn't want to fight in, let alone escalate aggression, I wasn't much interested to "nail the coonskin to the wall" as the President put it, but I heard about the GI Bill, and by golly, this war just might be my ticket to college. Mama said I was good with words and I didn't take kindly to all that double-talk the Company tried to sell us when any of the men got hurt working at the mine. Even the mayor thought I would make a good politician. I started thinking hard about becoming a lawyer. Yep, that's what I fixed my mind on.

When the day came to ship out, I remembered my mama's smile, but I could see her eyes shimmer like wet glass. I set down my black & brown suitcase and the green duffle bag, too, so I could hug her hard. My little sister, Katie Lynn, was cuddling her corn shuck doll that Mama fashioned with a frilled-up doily. The doll, dressed for a wedding, was just like the ones propped up on a wood-shiny shelf staring out the china closet glass in one of those fancy department stores. I kissed Sis on the cheek and tenderly placed another one—finger to lips—to her doll. I winked at her as I slipped out the door.

When I landed in Đà Nẵng, I could feel the devil in the air. Met some Kentucky boys from across the state, but I would soon learn about making friendships… they don't last in these jungles. Too many booby traps. I took shrapnel to my leg; tore it up real good. The doctors couldn't get the metal out, so I was left with a limp.

After the war, I went to college in upstate Illinois. The cold penetrated the metal in my leg, but I managed getting through my undergraduate classes, and even law school. I didn't set up practice in Chicago; I felt compelled to come back to the mountains, to the place I was born. Disability money would help me serve my hometown; Appalachian winters can be brutal to these kinds of wounds, too, but I could still stand against oppression.

And yes, I had to come back here to where the blood of my ancestors drenched the mountainside—just east of here on Ivy Mountain. And over yonder by the banks of the Licking River, where my kin were ambushed by militiamen when this great nation labored in birth. These fields of bluegrass are still stained. I could talk about *all* the wars in between… and all the feuds, too, but that would just be more politics. There was too much innocent blood spilled—humanity betrayed—to reduce it to that.

I had to return here, to where my own father's blood still soaks the coal dust under grave dirt, not because of any mine explosion, or because of any silent killer like black lung that got my Uncle Ronnie, or runaway trucks.

I had to return, not just to see Kentucky sunrises splashing crimson all over Rockhouse. I had to return to this place. *This* place, where the Bible's red-lettered words often spoke by Lincoln showed me the color of grace. I've come back to my roots to unshackle my soul, to stop its bleeding. This place is who I am; it's in my veins. I've come home, home, to blood.

Spring Cleaning by the Book with my Ex

Today I cleared my bedroom of books
hiding under the bed with cobwebs
and memories, a dozen gardening tomes
mounded under the slats of my futon's
frame, her nuclear systems training guides,
and a few classics like Jack London's
unabridged works. I think of a three-dog
night whenever *The Call of the Wild*
        comes to mind.
        It was cold
        last night and
I Saw Satan Fall bundled with *Gifts
of the Spirit*, not to mention a *Home
Medical Encyclopedia* (or two).
        Sometimes I dream
of numbers—no wonder,
with calculus under the mattress
and algebra that I don't use
          much anymore.
          How idiotic it is
an *Idiot's Guide to Wall Street*, or
my ex-wife's *Love Me Forever*
novel all piled together with
a broken
        Heart
of a Woman by Maya Angelou.
It doesn't seem right
to have *Marcella's Italian Kitchen*
on the *Bridges of Madison County*.
But love is sometimes built on trust
and food… and lust. Thank God
the floor under the bed is strong
enough to support the full library
          weight
of *Audubon's Birds of America*
with that huge pelican on the cover
        of a twenty-five pound book
measured in feet instead of inches.
Under another pile, *The Pelican*

Brief appeared with a collection
            of *Readers Digest*
Condensed Books along with lawyerly
dust mites haunting me as I rest
            at night and imagine
more mundane topics like the *Theory*
of Electromagnetic Wave Propagation.
Actually, that was one of my books
                stacked
                on top of
                The Civil War
Reader along with an *Act of Faith*,
a novel by Erich Segal.
After the swept-up dust settled
we cleared the air
            on who gets what
            book.

Part 2

My house

has no garage
no BMW or Mercedes Benz
just an old jalopy
              pick-up truck
with rusted chrome
and a pile of PBR bottles
in the back. My front
porch—split-rail punk wood
cages my daddy's rockin'
chair with a creak in its sway,
       but the lightning
bugs don't mind
and my old Bluetick hound
doesn't either.
When the midnight moon
ducks behind the hills
I slip into the kitchen
sit at the knotty pine table
I made for us a few years back,
where you served me
scrambled eggs & grits
with hickory smoked bacon
from a hog your uncle
stole. And black coffee
strong enough to keep me
standing on frost-cold
mornings; I still had to work
the cows and cornfields.
I think I'll have another
beer… I haven't slept
in our bed for a year
or two, the living
      room will do—
dreams don't come
as hard there.

Hoarding

This morning while getting ready
for a poetry workshop, the hotel TV
next to a stack of poems written
the previous day, shows a hoarder.

It seems to me she was collecting
dreams that she couldn't let go. I think
about a pile of boxes in my own
living room, and the columns

of notebooks in the garage. I struggle
to throw them out. In some, equations
from graduate school, lines yellowing
yet still with an elegance physicists

appreciate: the language of numbers;
images, even abstract, beautiful;
the music of symbols that dance
as poems in my head. In other notebooks

checkered or zebra'd, decorated
paisley black & white, or impressed
with purple and blue hexagons,
there are written poems, words buried

in the dusty pages with mold
& mildew growing between them.
They are waiting for their resurrection.

The house I lived in for thirty years

once rested under quiet starlight,
beneath a canopy of nighthawks
their songs punctuated by hoot owl
calls. Now, the lamppost by my window

is a perch for an artificial sun glaring
at the dark. O that sacred dark!

And the soft cadences of silence replaced
by hotrod traffic from a nearby racetrack
throwing up dust with the noise; the night
songs buried in the growl of engines.

The house I lived in for thirty years
once rested under blankets of floral esters,

the welcoming scents of hyacinth, rose
and lavender, as sweet as prayers. Now,
there's only stinking carcasses of road-kill
and stench from raccoon-raided garbage.

Skunks. Neighbors, always sneaking
back to take everything; what little I have

left of my dignity. The house I lived in
for thirty years was once my home,
but now is just an empty shell
to which I must return to every night

to sleep on pillows also emptied
of their dreams.

Condemned Property

After the woodborer beetle killed the pine trees
    in the backyard, the lumbermen felled them.
        Left remnants entwined with
barbed wire that used to fence the fields. The bugs
    moved out to plague another grove of trees.
        Now, new growth jungles the property.
Redbud and maple sprouts seem to make weeds
    look prettier than they are, they hide
        a garage, too, paint peeling on dry rot-wood.
The pit inside, once doubled-up for mechanic-ing cars
    and for the sheltering from tornadoes, is now full
        of old rainwash and debris that's fallen-in
shaken from shelves by an unforgiving night wind
    and maybe by my old worthless cat stalking mice
        she fails to catch.
But the old ceramic-lined satellite dish—once white,
    but now stained moss green—is still poised
        as if shouting its mildew voice to heaven
while a black walnut tree waves its branches
    over the horn of its mouth
        as if to hush it, to keep it from speaking
about everything it saw and heard in the rundown house
    when a man and his wife lived there
        before their yelling at each other withered
the vines, and the grasses that were once green too.
    Now, only ghosts remain, too tired to complain
        on who's going to mow the lawn—
even I don't listen to them anymore,
    and I still live there.

Yardwork

My sliding glass door—kitchen to backyard—is barricaded shut
with a piece of two by four wedged in the rail. A tattered beige
bedspread hides the outside world: a disappointed pin oak stands
over its branches fallen to the ground during last year's storms,
weathering; shadows cast by an unapproving sun, barge inside my
kitchen. The yard yells louder than any mockingbird, its unkempt
grass, scrub brush and maple saplings—together with poison ivy
and kudzu—clamor for attention. A baby blue swimming pool
from a local Wal-Mart butts up against the also-closed laundry
room door. A sea of leaves overflows its brim spilling on the
concrete patio. And by the brick and root walkway, a gray, molded-
plastic cat-house commandeered from a now long-gone dog, like
you, sits empty, its roof disheveled, also swept with fallen leaves. I
remember the Southern pines lining up as sentinels several rows
deep before the pine borer beetle got them. Pithy logs and
punkwood pieces are the only vestiges of their once looming
presence. A metal shed across the yard, a refuge for strays, a
temple for possums and raccoons, rusts in a distant memory of
praise and thanksgiving; no sympathy from a mulberry tree
stretching its barren arms overhead. It's liminal shadows, like
shaking fingers, on a deserted concrete birdbath, too stained to be
"yard sale-able."

So I close the "drapery," disallow anymore visitation except only
for faded light sifting through. But my eyes still hurt almost as
much as the brambles fisting in my heart.

There Once Was a Garden

Full of flowers and sweet fragrance.
Now, only hoarders: wild weeds
and briars, invasive vines, stubborn
brush, along with maple saplings
whose brothers have broken my
driveway, commandeered the yard,
converted it to "jungle" where snakes
can hide. No more a lush garden,
it has fallen to aggressive devil's snare.
I feel cursed like Adam remediating
his land, my hands blistered, now
humbled with no help, there is only
loneliness, and a lingering soreness
in my ribs.

Part 3

Song of the Mountains

She lives in the mountains.
       At dawn, she stirs under a quilt
             of stars, her eyes sparkle

in the alpine snow
       bright as an apricot sun—
             sweetens the horizon

with sugary light
       filtered through balsam firs
             and pine cones in her hair.

Her smiles mingle with
       uplifted forest and valley
             veiled in springtime phacelia.

Her breath,
       a hint of wintergreen
             mists the wonderland.

She herself is refuge
       a blessing to animals:
             tanagers and deer,

hoot owls and bears, whooping
       cranes on her lakes—blue
             gill and large mouth bass

peering through the underwater,
       shimmer up to the mirage
             heaven. The rainbow leaves

of fall on the surface—yellow hickory,
       scarlet maple…and copper
             basswood. I hear her sing:

the gurgling off-beat jazz
       of a cascade—her voice
             of many waters. The melody

of wind chiming through winter
        crystal or the percussion
                of branches swishing

their leaves. There is no mocking
        bird unsated, his two hundred songs
                practiced every day to the beat

of a pileated woodpecker
        on her poplar drum
                with cicadas' lilting rhythms

in the lazy summer.
        I love her
                classy mystery.

When that blue gray smoke
        gets in her eyes, she just winks
                and says I love you back.

Resurrection

The Tennessee sun dissolves into purple
lakes and the Great Smoky Mountains
send prayers to the other side of the valley.

Understory of lenticular clouds jigsaw the sky
and jagged mountain pines cut into the moon
falling on the coal black hills. The disk shreds,

shatters light. But the hoot-owl-night resurrects
hope for the dawn-washed hills hiding secrets,
their shame: mountains stripped

of their dignity; coffee-mud rivers sluicing dregs.

Water Ritual

Her warm rumors
always come with the wind
     and the oceans
give back their tears
to the sky,
     to their creator, salt
     traced drops coalesce
     as a breath from stars
while she's still whispering
like the wind. Inhales
     the joy, the sadness
     until she bloats
with impatience, flowers
to a fury before
     windows of heaven
     pull open.
Defenestrated, raindrops
rush with
     thunder, flash
     with anger, deluge
     the mountains,
till it too seeps
deep into earth,
     overflows
     rills and streams
rivering to oceans.
And the sun sparks
     the waves that undress
     before the light,
their soul susurrates
heavenward
     again.

Subterranean Poetics

The river writhes through narrow chambers, crisscrossing into reticulation of arteries mapping the heart of earth. For a moment, I'm smaller than a drop of that water dissolving through rock; smaller than a microbe propelling inexorably to the source of life, to the laughter of rain, to the brass-brilliant sun, to the hero of creation.

River Waking Mountains

The cock-of-the-walk hill in the shadows
of the mountains, roosts over farmland.
Its comb of purple-veined trees filter dawn:
soft, keratin yellow, bloodred translucence,
glory orange.

It's stone heart wrestles awake to the voice
of many waters dappled with the swish
of hope. No matter the accent of the streams
merging into one, they shout with the sun.

Star-filled Eyes

Orion always comes up sideways.
Throwing a leg up over our fence of mountains
—Robert Frost

He always wanted a telescope, so he spent all his insurance money
—the farm burned down, perhaps from that lightning storm last
month; spooked the cows in the barn, knocking over the kerosene
lamp, he said.

On a tripod, he mounts the telescope tube fashioned from well-
machined brass. It glints under stardust and tabernacles a silvered
mirror crafted from porthole glass ground smooth with fine grit.

In the eyepiece, a crescent moon gold-leafs the sky and fire-stars
glitter the night like gold dust. He chooses stars as his legacy.

As the telescope sifts the heavens, his eyes sparkle.

Allusions to Robert Frost's poetry are from Star-splitter and Choose Something
Like a Star

Slickrock Wilderness

After 'Trees' by Joyce Kilmer

The ascent into rich virgin forest
did not seem sacred, at least at first,

but it was. When Kilmer wrote about
the stately oaks and maples, no doubt

their striking kingly majesty, and some
so full of leaves—each one a poem

that bursts to life each lovely Spring,
those metaphors—those birds that sing

among the nestled branches into eves
of summer, the sultry breeze through trees.

They wait for Fall to fall and catch below
the scarlet sunlight, swaths of yellow

exploding in poetic words arranged, and full
of flavonoid, and carotene, and xanthophyll

that speak in a rustling, colorful tongue
to their creator, a psalm of love, a song

even into the withered cold when only
their crooked trunks are shown, and lonely

air blows through their limbs, yet still
they raise their arms on high—skies fill

with praise. They leave a legacy of poems
so they can live forever—their souls roam

rooted deep into earth. So when I touch the cold
bark of that old tree, its five-hundred-year-old

skin, I feel its heart pulse, hear it breathe—
susurrations of its words dropping soft as leaves.

Mountain Song

Maple, black gum and pawpaw sway
their spindly wood, young, in light wind.
Bright leaves splay filtered sun. South,
the mountains are quiet, to the north,
they cry the same mountain tune
I've heard fiddled for decades. The same
my daddy heard; his father, too. Blue grass
can't hide the scars striking land or men
made out of mud and muscle and blood.
Fall is beginning to wane and the brass
colored basswood already hardened here
their copper turning tinny brown. Clash
of leaves can't drum the truth away
that's buried beneath the taproots. Momma
would hum them as if they were sweet sour-
wood notes while hanging daddy's overalls
on the clothesline, still stained with coal
dust crammed into seams. And in cracks
of his leathered hands, face,
when he'd come home from working
Zeb Mountain long after stripping oak
and pine, dirt and rock, and coal
with the same black dust he'd breathe.
Coal scraped from mountains burdened
with false promises the Company made.
He paid, we paid, for that—earth reclaiming
him as so many others for the same debt.
Their souls inhabit the hills and the ground
trembles this time of year with their songs.
Maple, black gum and pawpaw sway
in quiet elegy under pulver of sixteen tons.

The Making of Steel

Crush ore into inch-round pieces:
magnetite, hematite, goethite, limonite,
or ferrous carbonate called siderite.
Geochemistry can sound so poetic.

Water-shower and wash away all
the clay, dirt, loam through weir and sieve.

Throw ore through throats of earthen furnaces
with charcoal fire inside. Roast it. Drive water
from the washings, and water tied-up in crystal
mineral. Expel impurities like sulfur.

Bellow air—increase heat. Let carbon ooze
from fuel into the molten mass smelted in
the mouths of furnaces. Upwind, watch them
breathe out gases from incomplete combustion.

Collect porous metal mixed with slag—
the bloom to be forged into wrought iron.
Heat, fold, beat, quench repeatedly. Then

injure beyond insult: tread on her air
with carbon footprints, then fashion
wrought iron into steel shovels
to spade earth, strip her of her coal,
feed her overburdened heart to river fish.

Before the invention of the blast furnace (1828), Kentucky built the first
charcoal iron furnace (1791) to make wrought iron, precursor of steel.

Death of a Mountain

Before the foundations of the world

He whispered life, breathed
a soul into the land, into every
living thing; everything was made

living.

But now, the ground shakes heavy
with machines—trees fall, the hill,
nude, flogged with chains,

scraped with massive shovels,
explosions churn up dirt. Heart
excavated until its pulse dwindles.

Handful of coal.

When they killed the spirit
of the mountain, the river swelled
with tears and the frogs drowned

in misery, and the mayflies
had no place to lay their eggs.
Even the rocks cried out

for the lilies of the valley.

And the streams, with the voice
of many waters, asked the mountain,
"I cannot sing, or breathe.

Why do you over burden me?"

And the lungless salamander
that lived on land and rill could not
soak in the air.

And the fish that used to swim
flicking fins against crystal clear swirls
now murks the mud.

Inside stripped-down mountains,
their ghosts, hundreds of them,
will moan the eulogy for centuries,

"How long?"

Wild River

And if the church is there beside the river
Could I go back and find where momma lay
—'Tennessee 1949' (Gobel and Drumm)

Rounding river's bend, my eyes bridge water
and steam plant, drift to an old Appalachian story
told on a wrinkled Barking Legs Theater program

floating in the backseat breeze of my Ford.
I grab the brown paper, fold it in half and scribble
a few words into empty spaces about the sun

and how it smears the horizon in early April
over the Tennessee River. And about Kingston's
coal plant belching gas through its tall stacks

oblivious to last December's sludge slide
when the berm had broken under weight
of neglect. Fly ash coal murking deep into river

graves, stirs mud on the stars and the forgotten
farmers working good bottomland for generations,
their murmurs muted by dirty waters. I still hear

the rampage of the dam river-flood, the drowning
voices just beneath the wrinkled surface
pitted with blue-gray tears—a past reflection

scoured by the late afternoon sun to a still
platinum finish.

Lake Sign

The sign off Tallassee's Calderwood Highway, smudged with purple humor—the smeared out word *No*—teases passersby: *Alcoholic Beverages Allowed: Warning* and continues saying something about catfish. The rest of the sign, illegible, begs that the *Catfish are not to be eaten* for they are drunk. A sobering thought. Who would've thought when the Tennessee Valley Authority dammed up the damn river that the catfish would be in so much protest. I suppose it might have been because of the messed-up river bottoms to where the catfish were sluiced into. Yet, not because of sunken, mud-churned farmland or layered silt or even the murky history of waterlogged towns, but rather by the ghosts of the dead buried there in Cherokee gravesites. Their names are etched on the watery silence, all of them: Chota, Tanasi, Toqua, Tomotley, Citico, Mialoqua, Tuskegee. Native Americans lost their lands to the settlers (who stole them from the tribal nations), who in turn lost them to the landowners whose interests were anchored in dam power—hydroelectric—that flood-washed their history, and dignity. Only a haunting remains.

Today, some picnickers stumbling on the rocks spill their beer in the river-lake intoxicating the fish. They laugh.

I cry.

Part 4

Aubade

A paling purple lavenders the dawn,
sky brightens with choruses of scarlet,
persimmon and chrysanthemum light

before the gold notes sift through
the dark morning noise.

Lazy gray swish of a wake-up shower
on a tin roof. Pitter-patter percussion.

Syncopated beats jazzing with the percolator,
B-flat thrums mix with the drumming
of a pileated woodpecker.

Orioles, cardinals and Carolina wrens
celebrate with symphony.

Then there's Mozart
                 with the beignets
and allegro movements

of my pen scrawling across paper
ending with consonantal rhyme
of *Good morning* as a song

inside my heart full of sibilant and liquid
string-chords: *Sweetheart, I love you—*

the harmony of your smile,
                 the crescendo of your kiss.

Breakfast at Midnight

We are hungry after we kissed
all night in our driveway, and later
at an IHOP, the host splits our order
—two large pancakes & eggs—
places them in black Styrofoam boxes.

We eat our midnight snack in the car
still running because we had to jump
the battery; it completely discharged
because we left the tailgate open
to let the cool honeysuckle breeze in
and hear the swish of pines where
spring's first fireflies flashed together
with the cool gauzy light of stars—
green scintillations sparking the haze
of a hot mayapple moon.

I lean across the console, whisper
something holy, then caress her
face. We kiss. That salt-sweet savor
—bacon & maple syrupping our lips—
lingers
        even after fifty years.

The Last Rose

In the palm of leaves, still-pink petals
scroll tight trying to hold onto summer.

They unwind in autumn night, one last fling
among lovers. Sky, in twilight's passion,

does not blush. Night air softly kisses
the velvet petals. They whorl inside

holding themselves tight against
the coming chill. And the thorns

have not softened. A rose is *a rose
by any other name* is

you embracing me, me wrapping around you
like last summer, after the freeze.

Italicized reference is from Shakespeare's *Romeo and Juliet*

Soon the Sugar Maples Will Bleed

The hoot-owl moon listens
to the serenade of trees:
Pawpaw with its rocking
limbs in rhythm with wind,
percussive swish of leaves
—a lullaby. Sweet gum
scents the breeze, hemlocks
and oaks rattle, but not
a quake among the poplars.

No fig trees for forbidden lovers
wrestling under firs on a soft sod
mat of evergreens; mourning
doves singing their elegy…
The thorn bush quiet
                              for now.

A Hundred Shades of Green Blaze the Trail

Greenbrier Pinnacle Trail
Great Smokey Mountains National Park

Luscious wet, green where April's trillium
and fields of phacelia adorn the rumpled terrain.

Spackled light through a parasol of poplar leaves
illumines the tender mayapple green, and ferns

that feather the escarpments. Birch and basswood
offer their own rich hues. The air is delicious

with sassafras overshadowed by hickory and oak,
the understory full of wintergreen's teaberry.

I sit on a log plush with moss, green with
invitation, you next to me. We share spearmint

candy watching the peregrines. Your hazel green eyes
enchant the forest, but blaze my heart—a flame
                    azalea opening to you.

The Path Taken

The sweetgum trees line up under the angled sun
their shadows in tight rows haunt the trail. The faint cries
of passionflowers—complaints—when I ask them
if I had taken the right road. So what if I'm the third
person today with a troubled voice. Even when I ask
my creator, S/He remains silent. Now loudly, the flowers
proclaim God always whispers. But I am down and deeply
deaf to those susurrations, I can only hear the quake
of my own heart. I suppose solitude and loneliness
overwhelm the lively green in the forest, maybe
it would've been better to have taken another road,
a path where stratus gray doesn't pile up but be supplanted
with aquamarine—the sky and distant trees smiling
with a light-filled palettes sunshining in symphony with
my transforming thoughts—not tainted banana-fish yellow
that has drowned so many in a bone-splitting second
of a .38 cracking the air, the ear—but something
golden like the *yellow wood* looking *as far as I could*
to see shadows of the past, pass by. The trees, though
still murky with indigo, have the promise of scarlet
because, because, because, because the yellow-brick yellow path
is stained with yet a more-emerald smile under my feet:
To where it bends *in the undergrowth. I'm off to see*
where my *Wonderful* God is leading me.

Italicized words come from the poem "The Road Not Taken" (Robert Frost)
and the song lyrics in *The Wizard of Oz*, "Follow the Yellow Brick Road"
(Lyman Frank Baum/Paul Tietjens)

Wilderness

Sheltered in place sounds nurturing, protective, but this manmade wilderness is not interested in my survival. Depression doesn't give a damn either; it won't stop plaguing me. When I've had enough, I leave with a salty blur in my eyes and drive away to the park because I know I can talk to the mountains—on the trail, my feet touch earth, and the earth touches me. I am connected to this marvelous creation, and to the creator. I feel a presence wrap me like a hug.

I ponder out loud, but only hear the echo of myself in the haunting stillness, yet even the rocks thrust out their arms and cry out in praise. I look up, past the azure, imagine the myriad of stars that I cannot see, but hear their proclamations as loud as the psalmist had voiced in the Scriptures. I have so many questions; try not to argue with myself about whether I have purpose or not. But all I want to right now is to know when I can hug the people I love. Will I die from the virus before I can kiss her again? A broken heart is just as fatal.

I pull myself back into the splendor that surrounds me, every imaginable shade of luscious green borders the trail, along with the boisterous colors of spring. The flowers are as numerous as those stars—a galaxy of wildflowers—phlox, bluets, asters, and daisies, even trillium with all its holy symbolism; wild geranium and daylilies bowing to the orchestra of nature; and white-fringed phacelia with its delicate elegance—their names are blessed among the flora that grace this time of solitude. Their scent is a sweet prayer merging with mine.

I kneel by a stream, soft sod beneath my aging knees, listen to the gurgle in the crystal purity of water, in its rampage over dark gray limestone mossy with secrets, and try to decipher their answers in the static hiss of collapsing bubbles. I concentrate on the sunken leaves scattered on the bottom of a quieter pool at the edge of an eddy—fragments of mica-glitter and rust-layered shale surely must render a hint of answers hiding there.

Perhaps it's in the sanctity of the pines among the warblers and the wrens—Carolina's song pulling the loneliness out of me.

Everything beautiful in them is truly given. I am no poor man, but blessed in the company of angels—these messengers sent to comfort, put my hurt on their wings and take it to the One above the clouds, beyond the stars, who will replace it with uncanny hope. A speckled brown sparrow lands a few feet from me and flits and flutters in the thistle as it cocks its head this way and that, as if it's listening to the breath from the white dove that lives in the spaces between my susurrations giving it instruction for my benefit.

A breeze lifts from the quiet air, stirs the sycamore leaves, and the rhododendron quivers in anticipation. Something inside me understands the language of trees yet my heart moves to the rising pathos in resonance with Barber's *Adagio for Strings* playing in my mind. Despite the sadness, there's a beauty I feel more than understand.

I walk back down the trail, my feet, not as heavy; my heart, lighter. There's a rhythm to all of this in these times of change. Ferns edging the trail remain green regardless of the weather. I crane my neck up once more. A few clouds are gathering and I taste the wetness in the air; the blue is fading for silvery gray but the sun is not hiding from me anymore, no matter how dark the clouds turn. And when the rain comes, it will drop soft as mercy.

Rebecca

<u>Born 1801</u>
Rebecca Angela Smith
Porter's Creek, TN
Daughter of John and Sarah Smith
German-Irish immigrant farmers
who grew sweet onions
next to wild trillium
and fields of white phacelia
where the creek runs clear
as babies' tears.
Anchored there
pads of floating
watercress
peppery green
soft as rain—cool buttery
bitter taste that spring.
All her little smiles and kisses, too
a lifetime between each one
all forty-two million heartbeats
consumed
her breath.
<u>Died 1802</u>

Woodcarving

          Grandfather's knife
levers its burden into the soft heart
of a chunk of evergreen, biting deep
into wood, resurrecting
          pain with every carve.
Every time dawn glazes
the grass's dew for the last twenty years,
he sits in a rocker, inside the screened-in
porch, shaves off curls of cedar—peelings
          from his whittler's blade
falling to the pinewood floor—shapes it
into doe and fawn, the pleasant scent
of memory. Grandmother whispers
          in his ear, gently
he raises his frail body and struggles
to the kitchen table set for three. Coffee
percolates in a blue porcelain pot, bitter
dregs still manage to pour through.
          Outside the cabin
window, a mother and speckled fawn
graze, their necks poised over a thick
patch of Dutch white clover.
          The early sun catches
the familiar glistening in their eyes,
the way hazel brown is refulgent
in morning light—just like that of his
          daughter, granddaughter
before the accident. He moans, cries deep
into the wilderness, longing
for another brief visit.

Dead Logs in the Stream

There's always peace in the forest
and the trees don't argue much
      with me

not even the shagbark hickory
though there are these haunting

whispers in the advective breeze
over sassy waters, which always gurgle
      their words.

They are quick to wash secrets away.
I've come to spill mine

but the lightning had slashed down
the table mountain pine, toppled it

into the fierce stream a few years back.
Slick rocks sheltered the tree from certain
      disintegration

before a canopy of yellow fungi rooted
themselves in the misty seams.

I knelt in the trail to pray by the pagoda
mushrooms, listened to their voice
      crying
      in the wilderness.

They pled, *the dead, the dead*
logs are in the deep stream.
      Don't jump.

Engulfed

I am thinking of you and the last time we kissed.

Windshield wipers set on slow in the gray drizzle. Rain-fog steaming up from the wet asphalt slick with smeared oil. A tired John Deer tractor hauling a round of hay, hulks in misty shadows in the middle of the bridge, it's red taillights burned-out. My horn blares a B-flat-G annoyance, as if that could slow down and stop my hundred-forty horses. I swerve verging on the median; brakes lock, tires spit gravel before the guardrail mangles on impact flipping the boxy van. It careens down the steep embankment, tumbling in a slow dance with death. The cold creek, deep with remorse, swallows my vintage Chevy van. Water gushes in. Soon it will smother me. No strength in my legs to kick out the windshield pressing hard against the murky green. Topside lights dimming like a watery moon. Even my fleeting thoughts are trapped, emptied of everything, except of you. You, smiling, waving me goodbye; the scent of your hair still impressed in my nostrils, the taste of you on my lips even after all these years. My heart beats for desperate air, longing for breath, your breath.

Baby, I'm coming home.

Carolina Special

I truck
to a joint near New Market, Tennessee
simply longing a barbecue
sandwich of hot pulled pork
or smoked brisket steaming
on dishes. Oak smoke curls
       into
my nostrils; my teeth and tongue
ready for the meat with a special
Carolina sauce, a bit pungent yet
sweet. But the mural on the wall,
no longer staying silent, screams
       through
the paint—a loud and plaintive
cry among the hills of southern
Appalachia hidden in the trees
that trade colors for mysteries
       of
the fall. Two fast trains
hurry with their secrets
sleeping in Pullman cars.
They roll on tracks slick
       with
sharp memories
bleeding into an
uncertain future
chugging home

On September 24, 1904, the Carolina Special out of Chattanooga and local train No. 15 out of Bristol, due to miscommunication, collided on the main line of the Southern Railway by New Market, TN, at over 100 mph killing and/or injuring over 100 people.

Part 5

Black

Shadows in the predawn // Pine tar walls of the Company Store / The shade of their souls // Coal-black coffee / Your porcelain cup // Murky streams under a new moon / The full moon in Braille // Crow's wings in starlight // Obsidian, onyx, ebony and hematite / gold without light // Acetylene lamps starved of oxygen // Miner's blood caked mud-hard dry // Canary's eyes after carbon monoxide poisoning // Papa's lungs in the x-rays // The sound of your voice falling into a deep shaft / swallowed by a black hole in the ground // Death mixed with dirt, ash and dust // The color of emptiness

Nuggets of Coal

I am stardust, I am golden
—Joni Mitchell

They shut down
the Number 2 Willow mine.
Coal piled up at the entrance
now covered with new dirt
and dark green Kentucky grass
scattered with canary yellow
poppies—seeds black-as-coal
giving birth to golden petals
to reclaim land. In chambers
below flowers, sulfur-yellow
birds sang through dust-choked
air. Echoes remain. Clean shafts
of sun, aurum cores of light,
might never have augered
the shiny coal. That carbon
along with gold once fired
in distant suns, now lays dark
like embers melting into shadows
just like the coal cars and rails
disappearing into the abyss
along with the men who lusted
for nuggets of gold. Down there,
their bones lie in the black dust
along with unglittered gold.

undying

let the spirits of the dead
slip through God's fingers
| | re-enter your bodies | | feel
yourselves quiver exhaling
black dust | | unchoke coal
from your throats | | watch
tons deluge from walls | |
ceiling | | move away from
the final entrance | | step
back into the elevator | |
start laughing halfway up
the shaft | | at a joke about
mine safety and waiting for
someone to unkill the bill
for more inspections | |
try to forget the undying
allegiance | | laugh some
more | | slip past the door
| | put your helmet & gear
in the corner of your
shanty and unbreak your
wife's heart | | unpress
your lips hard to hers | |
sit at the kitchen table
| | unswirl the coffee
from the cup | | untaste
the eggs before they're
returned to pan to shell | |
don't pray with your wife
| | slip back into bed | |
untouch her | | don't listen
to the rooster | | don't let
the dawn in

At a Writer's Retreat Near a Coal Mining Town

Sed fugit interea, fugit irreparabile tempus.
(Meanwhile, the irreplaceable time escapes)
—Virgil, *Georgics*

The holly tree, bigger than any I have ever seen, looms over the backyard garden; pinches sky with pinned waxy leaves. I stand on the hill. Study every rock, every tree lining the walkway to the house. This place is as silent as English ivy creeping up the escarpment.

> *As silent as dirt that once was here before*
> *it was stripped for its coal 30 years ago*

Gnarled dogwoods—too early to show blossoms—pray. Their naked branches scratch sky layered as slate above the artist's bungalow: steel beams, tongue-n-groove floors, old glass sagging under its own weight. A small study with just enough room for kitchen, and a short bed.

> *But not as short as the hard pine cot*
> *in the board and batten mining town shack*

When it rained a few years ago, the copper roof pinged as if sand swished on it; but now, its bright metal has weathered to dull gray-green; drops simply thud when clouds bear their heaviness. I peer through windows, pensive, resolute, mesmerized by a stone sculpture in the verdant microcosm. Its base, chiseled with angelic faces, one for each corner of earth.

> *I imagine like the ones on stone cold miners*
> *when the shaft caved in; prayers chiseled on their lips*

The round stone, overlaid with brass, is scribed with Roman numerals, as if a clock for kings, its face watching a zodiac of gods pass by. A black scorpion gnomons the heavens, splits the gold disc in the sky, splays the shadow of fleeing sun on the dial caught between its pincers, as if to scepter time. An untimely walkway-limestone had fallen on the scorpion, killing the way it

70

tried to hold hostage the passage of time. At the base of the pillar, a purple crocus blooms.

All gravestones are untimely
in our eyes, whether marble or coal

Some Say It's the Moonshine

Some say
my talk ain't hillbilly
enough to call me
Appalachian.
   But I'm poor.
My clothes, those
hand-me-downs,
are clean
   despite farm dirt
and straw—
a strand stuck between my teeth,
and yes, some are missing
in my smile
   but what you don't see is
my heart. Momma says
it is kind, but heavy
as a mountain, holy
as the flowers on it, blooming
words that praise
   my culture
coursing through my veins.
There's coal dust there too.
Some say there's nothing good in that,
but like papa, who worked hard
to care for us, I breathe in
   its blackness
press it hard
in my lungs, somehow
   make it diamond.

Part 6

A Dry Stone Wall at Antietam

No mortar to bind the dry stack:
ties, risers, capstones dug out of
earth with pick, levered with a
> digging bar or shovel. Wall erected
> with brawn of rock-fence men:
> cattle keepers, homesteaders,
farmers and defending soldiers.
But the hard truth here: limestone
and flint and bones, riddled and
> chipped with musket balls, stood
> as stone wall barricades, memorials.
> Weathering cannot erase the stain
of war; rain cannot wash away
the ghosts, or any of their spilled
honor, or any of their sacred duty
> soaked deep into scarred ground.
> There was no mortar to bind
> the dry stack, no cement
>> but blood.

Inspired by a calendar photograph of a Dry Stone Conservatory Workshop,
Fayette County, Kentucky

75

Antietam National Battlefield Museum: A Poem

I

A hot breeze sweeps through the Civil War
artillery, its black metal rendered innocent
with sky blue paint among the yarrow and larkspur,
jessamine and hollyhocks and sweet ubiquitous
abelia all shooting up around the cannon
anchored in grass; its barrel pointing
               to a distant mountain,
               to where a previous day's battle
raged a hundred fifty years ago.
Scent of black powder long since wisped away.

I am blinded by the glare off the barrel, but still see
smoke from the gun, and its fire; still hear its roar,
and cries from wounded men.

I open my eyes and shake my head; pray
the cannon and its noise would disappear.
Stark images remain, as does the smell
of sulfur. It chokes my memory.
But among the those flowers
there's a sweeter sense of peace.

Inside the museum, a lanky park ranger
stretches a smile to welcome me, and my wife;
takes a couple of bucks, and promises
an experience we will not forget.

Dimly lit rooms shadow the past,
a past that we wish was never there.

The exhibits, mostly Union, are scattered
throughout the building with some
Confederate memorabilia, too. I disdain that word—
it's as if tourists are being entertained
with our battered history, its awful wares on display.
It sickens me. But the past itself sickens me more.

I parade slowly in front of every exhibit,
stopping to study each item. I cannot touch
any of them with my hands, but I hold them
in reverence with my eyes. There's holiness here,
I can feel it. I know this is hallowed ground.
I cannot say exactly why
this place, at this time, is any different from
any other battlefield. But it's much more
than just a place where blood had spilled.
It's something grabbing hold of my insides
and shaking the hell out of me.

My wife asks if I'm okay. I stutter a yes
but she knows I'm lying. I try to coax the words out
but I can barely articulate what's on the sign,
the letters and numbers distorting
through the glassy wetness in my eyes.
My mouth moves to bring the words closer to my lips,
but they keep getting stuck in my throat.

There's a keen sense of bereavement; I cannot begin
to explain. My heart pulses, one beat for each soldier
who had fallen, and my heart is sore with grief
for hours. Inside myself, I cry through the numbness.

My head still bowed, I stare at the numbers
I just had read, my voice wavers out loud,
"I feel as though I was there. No. I *know*
I was there on the battlefield in command,
yet I don't know the color of my uniform."
My wife simply listens. There's a heaviness
I cannot lighten—

                    not then for my men,
                    or now, for myself.

II

Behind the glass, the sword and sabers
and bayonets still rusted from countless rains,
are laid in the case, their dirt-brown surfaces
cannot hide the dried blood.

Uniform-stuffed manikins appear to puff out
their chests, and display their brass metal buttons
and combed cotton that must have belonged
to an officer.

Early in the war, many of the boys-made-men
only wore farm clothes, some tattered blue,
others a drab gray—on both sides of the battle.

In these picture frames, all are young men in sepia
or in black & white. Museum lights glint off
photograph glass, and the smiles of those young men:
Union boys dressed in Ivy League-like clothes—
neatly pressed trousers, crew cut sweaters. Their clean-
-shaven faces showing boyishness. On those glassy
portraits, their innocence and romantic notions
of duty and honor, courage and patriotism
would soon-enough be shattered—these young men
wore blue in their hearts that would soon bleed red.

Bullets—neatly arranged as Stone Age artifacts
shaped as blunt, lead-gray cones, their back ends
ridged with three or more grooves to stabilize
bullet's flight path all the way to its fleshy target—
look so innocent. Science is beautiful, ballistic,
but the engineering is crude, especially for those
bullets on impact tumbling inside the body, tearing
tissue and sinew, splintering bone, severing arteries
and limbs. I never understood the civility of fighting
in the Civil War—soldiers lining up in columns
of long rows, facing each other less than a hundred
yards apart with one-shot muskets, then firing
their primitive instruments of war at each other.

I suppose it was patriotism of some kind
that gave those boys the fortitude to stand
and the courage to fall for what they believed,
or for what their commanders had ordered.

Do you suppose they were deafened

by the sound of guns, by the loud thumps
of their falling bodies full of holes?

I shift my eyes to a mural
stretching across one of the walls.
The light is dim, but the scene clear,
depicting one of the engagements on that day.

I unfold a pamphlet stuffed in my back pocket
that the ranger gave me earlier, the crinkling
of paper is too loud for the solemnity of this place,
yet I am deafened by the words I have yet to say.

The mural, just silent paint on the wall,
echoes beyond the silence, beyond cannon roars,
beyond musket fire, and the yells of Rebels
and Yanks. I force my eyes to the printed words
on that paper moist from the sweat of my fingers.

As I try to read, pressure builds in my sinuses
and my head aches. My rapidly-filling eyes
dilate just to focus, to read the history.
It shouldn't be this hard, but I am barely able
to articulate the words, as if I am drunk.
My mouth dries, lips quiver, and the words
burn my throat. They slur as I try to read
the staggering number of American casualties.
You'd think I would have gotten over that
by now. I've read those same words hanging
on a sign so many times before.

III

Inside a curtained room, James Earl Jones' magnificent voice
booms in a documentary film about the historic Battle of
Antietam in Sharpsburg, MD. His intonations of the account, the
tenor of his heart, speak a truth beyond the facts.

He doesn't have to state all the battle details. Re-enactors in their
engagements led by the Union forces are clear enough, and the
carnage in that late summer of 1862 is self-evident. It was the

bloodiest day of the Civil War with casualties as high as 28,000.
How many of them fell from staggering incompetence?

IV
We leave the museum, begin a self-guided tour
of the battlefield

—the microcosm and macrocosm of it all, overwhelming,
like the range of magnitudes in a science class video
that I show my students called the "Powers of Ten."
It gives a sobering perspective—the enormity
and minisculeness of things—

but this battlefield experience is not about galactic
super structures or quarks in sub nuclear world:

Zoom out five, fifty, five hundred, five thousand feet so you
cannot tell, when you look down, the forest from the trees, the
generals from their men, the blue from the gray. They scurry like
ants on a hill and through the gaps; and smoke from cannons
appears as small wispy clouds; and the blood drenching the fields,
its red blends with the bright sunset.

Zoom in until those insect-like dots take form. And the unmoving
ones metamorphose into dismembered bodies—arms, legs, heads
—strewn among the corn fields. Move in closer so you can see fire
through the musket smoke; bayonets glinting silver and crimson;
hand-to-hand combat; young men who are really boys with that
scared-as-shit look on their faces, even on the dead ones
contorted to almost-smiles.

V
Six months later, I am driving through east
Tennessee with it's own rich history
from the Civil War, I review a lecture

in the blank slate of my mind about the ballistics
of cannon fire for my physics class.
A whoosh of air violently jostles my car

80

at the same instant I hear an explosion.
A tractor-trailer rig flying down the hill
in the opposite lane, blows a tire just as it passes me.

Debris scatters all around me; smoke plumes
and dirt sprays upward as the truck crashes
through thick galvanized steel.

At that speed, the truck is no match for the guardrail.
My rear view mirror shows the wreckage in progress—
truck careening down the steep embankment

into a deep ditch. Blunt force trauma to the driver
is what I think out loud. All of this calamity
subsumes me. That tsunami of explosive wind

blows me into the past, onto a battlefield,
my commanding officer yelling "Watch out!"
Hot gases recoil the cannon. I jam another

twelve pounder into the maw of that fire-blowing
dragon, deafened by its roars all day until the sun
had set.

Falling
Leaves

They might be called trees of righteousness

Poplars twirl parallel to ground
Cupping air as they softly land

Maples see-saw their way down
Stabbing sky with serrated leaves

> In the palm of their hands, fingers curl
> Others point to those still quivering
> On the branches, waving goodbye in the wind
> In a *garment of praise for the spirit of heaviness*

Hickory spins about its leaf-stem
Veins suspend blood in centripetal motion

Some leaves quake and flutter—it all depends
On how much sugar and xanthophyll
On how much rain, when the cold

Snaps their will
One last radiance of color
Their surrender

> To battle
> To the onset of brittle shells
> To the mottle and brown

Give unto them beauty for ashes
the oil of joy for mourning

They willingly return to soil
To their place of birth

> These souls
> Of trees

Quotations from Isaiah 61:3

I always carry my words and the sounds of my life

in the mouth of my soul, in the pockets of my heart,
but there's always a certain rhythm to death
as in the phugoid cycles of falling leaves, how they thwart
gravity to lift them up, and in their one final breath,

the rasp on grave dirt, eulogy of rustled spirits, brown-gray
voices point to mother's arms that once held them high.
The same wind that lullaby'd them in sweet summer sway
and thrummed harps—thin limbs strung in aeolian sky,

green leaves intoning wind—a chlorophyll of sound,
now brings the sugar-poor air of winter singing psalms,
dirges of night, this music of earth where hope is found,
transforms them to be one with themselves. Those B-flat hums

of death metronome the crumbling of atoms, is what I take
—my symphony of life, my resurrection in death. I shake.

I am that leaf.

The title is a line from the article, "10 Ideas That Could Save American Poetry,"
Seth Abramson, *The Huffington Post* (February 20, 2017)

Ode to Sunflowers

Love turns aside the balls that round me fly
Lest precious tears should drop from Susan's eye
—John Gay

Your sun-filled petals daisy chain
the wind, and your hearts sway
through history. O Black-eyed Susan—
Maryland's flower that booms past
remembrances—not a speck of red
on your garments adorning grassy
lanes at Sharpsburg, its cannons too;
your tender shoots would celebrate,
your September blooms aroma the air,
cover the stench of sulfur, memories
of war. You encourage, inspire justice.
Your language, symbols, your words
rest on the nightstand next to the Bible.
At Appomattox, you offered peace
that was bedded that spring, and soon
the fields would no longer be exploding,
except for flowers, your lovely flowers.

---

i. The Black-eyed Susan became Maryland's State flower in 1918
ii. Sharpsburg, MD was the site of the bloodiest one-day battle of the Civil
    War—the Battle of Antietam (September 17, 1862)
iii. The Rudbeckia flower was nicknamed from a reference in a poem by John
    Gay (1685-1732)

Dirt Bags

A busted vacuum in city breeze—dust blowing with the windy breath || of politicians and the sanctimonious || words of legalistic preachers, stiff as flint || or carpetbaggers that would stiff the southerner in a flash with their own kind of song-and-dance || real dirtbags—not just the unkempt—but the morally bankrupt ones like the pimps on Hill Street Blues || But is this real || or surreal dirt? || The soil beneath your feet? || Physics is indifferent || Stepping on the pulver of shaly sandstone || doesn't offer a coefficient of restitution close to one as you walk || that might spare shock to your knees || to your heart || Yet there's nothing firm left to stand on || You smirk gravity has hijacked rust-dirt and coal dust || Perhaps the rivers becoming overburdened pulled the dirt into them along with any ethical conscience || now dirty enough || to thwart life.

Speculators

Appalachia during Reconstruction

They wielded the same kind of dirty carpetbags
I saw down South full of dust-filled promises.

What were they planning to do with all the *worthless*
land they'd be taking off my hands? I didn't hear

the scarlet tanagers or the pine warblers
miss the notes in their songs as I signed the papers.

I didn't smell deceit on the ink-and-must stained
documents… only the sweet honeysuckle outside.

But soon my ears would burn when I heard
the truth, my mouth left acrid, my tongue stumbling

on the cheap texture of lies. Blinded. I couldn't see
the sun setting behind the grieving mountains—

shadows veiling their purpled faces. River babbling
regret down below. I know it won't wash my sin away.

Just like they swindled us out of our common land—
the rocky wilderness for timber, coal, and tan-bark

with chicanery and fancy laws on *corporate enclosure,*
they'd be digging out the ore; draining gas & oil

and the hearts and minds of simple mountain people.
I should've known when they came in those lawyer suits

wearing those uppity smiles, swinging satchels with their
promise-me-the-moon-but-give-me-the-gutter looks.

Edge Effect

When the sun ducks below the folds of the mountains
I can hear it's crimson-throated song purpling the sky.

In unison, with the gurgle of once pristine streams,
the tanagers and wrens voice their loneliness for clean

hope. In the edges of where I encroach the sanctity
I kneel to hear their prayer. Each one crumbled

as a dry leaf under my foot.

Bear Stories

The Great Smoky Mountains National Park

Newfound Gap Road cuts through the heart
of the Smokies—deep woods solitude, a foot-trail away.
In the Chimney's Picnic area, a fork of water roars.
Into water's rush, slab-shaped boulders had tumbled
a billion years ago. Ice clear eddy pools lie nearly still,
filled with pebble limestone and quartz scaled with rust.
Brown oak leaves float and interlock into a collage
of zoo shapes.

From the sunlit side, rocks jut out from laurel banks,
light falling below the ridge pines—needles knifing the sun
whose rays spike into starbursts—I ponder about
the woman who sat here last week, and about the bear
with that star-fire reflecting in its forest eyes. Half-blinded
by glare, she could still discern the silhouette of that bear
… She shouldn't have run. She shouldn't have screamed.

~~~

Northern red oak branches smoked on a wood-coal fire
seared a sirloin tip roast laced with wine and herbs.
Fat dripped into flames. Peppercorn & garlic licked air,
and the tongues of nearby bears. They came. Panicked
friends rushed to the safety of their automobiles. I stayed
holding on to the precious meat in my trembling hands.
Funny thing. One bear looked straight at me, stood up
on its hind legs, sniffed air, then four-footed it to picnic
garbage cans. It rummaged for a more appetizing meal.
Bells collaring its broad furred neck, simply jostled
as if chimes announcing his cool November dinner.
No one screamed but stayed hunkered down in their cars.
I stood still as stone.

~~~

I thought I imagined the sound of bells in the deep woods
while hiking Gabe's Mountain Trail. I didn't know that a bear
tagged with bells was stalking me. It remained covert in brush
while growling intimidations. *Don't Feed the Bears*, a voice
inside that didn't alarm me soon enough. I shouldn't have
thrown my half-eaten sandwich; I lobbed it high into kudzu
in the direction of all that grumbling. Hickory-smoked bacon
on an onion roll with cream cheese, sprouts & cucumber,
and some salt-and-peppered spring onions—a diversion
to facilitate escape. By the commotion, the high-pitched grunts
from the brush, I couldn't tell if it liked those onions. I wanted
to run, but didn't, instead I walked as fast as hell, praying loudly
without a sound.

White Lightning

Bardstown, Kentucky
September 2015

Jim Beam, that bourbon whiskey, still
in a warehouse when lightning struck.
Fire-gutted walls gave way to deluge
of 800,000 gallons of liquor, burning
all the way down the throat of the
mountain side to a retention pond.
This lake of fire—swill and swirl—
caught the thunder of a devil-mean
tornado. It sucked up the fire liquid
into its own mouth.

Hundreds of drunken fish stared.

Based on a true event early in September 2015:
Firenado https://youtu.be/LKTNMbEoOKE

High Definition

I sink into my leather chair,
half drift off on soft cushions,
flip on the remote and pop
the aluminum tab off a Bud.

First, The Weather Channel:
the Gulf, with its typical August
hurricane churning Cuban waters
from green to battered gray.

Same old-same old.

I switch to Channel 42, Ah!
All that jazz and drum snares,
syncopated trumpets—music
washing over me, I float

in that sea of leather.
I take another sip of beer,
suspend in high definition—
in that silk of sound

before another damned crash
of infomercials on my ears.

I click over to ESPN:
Saints against Tampa Bay
Buccaneers. It's raining
and the score is tied at halftime.

The Clydesdales' white-capped
hooves beat mud and the screen
blinks & rasters turning them
into red brown blurs on chartreuse,

So I switch to CNN, to another
part of the world in wake

of that hurricane—African coast.
I hear pleas for aid. Emaciated
children drowning
with hunger.

They are gasping to breathe

the last air of hope. I crush
the empty beer can. Stuff the last
of that Po Boy into my mouth
and turn-off the plasma TV.

I stare at the blank screen

after the electric discharge
crinkles air as if some static
hum dissolves like beer froth
collapsing on glass, sliding down

the wall of an empty mug.

Part 7

Chiseled in Stone

They say Nature just is

that it doesn't hear its own song from a hymnbook
in the rocks, no rhyme, or even reason, just history.

Yet I hear its music written among the sheets
of shale, carboniferous pages of club pines and palms,
ferns 350 million years old.

Fossil impressions on the hardcover
of rocks give a hint of authorship.

Limestone notes an ancient sea full of
stems—sea lilies—and brachiopod shells—
tomes of stone imprinted with literary pages

of time, the sifting of Miocene sands revealing
character & plot lasting until today under oceans.

From wine-darkened seas, with its Silurian waves
turning pages, to a watery desk full of pearly sea pens
and black quills of urchins dipping into murex ink.

I walk with my head through inky depths, my arms
trying to fathom all the meaning I see written.

Some letters are sharp as shark teeth, others smooth
as whalebone. I read the stories, even the hard
metamorphic ones— they change me.

The words are crystal whether in a book
of mica with its glitter and promise, or scorched

by volcano fire, with vugs of amethyst
that purple its soul and sapphire its heart.
Each moment, a poem.

What thoughts from the mind of God
are spelled here?

The Walnut Street Bridge

Reflections on Monday, March 19, 1906

It was on the cusp of spring, like now, when I painted this 1890 bridge. I stood on the southern shore of the Tennessee, and my canvas caught the filtered light through the nimbus clouds. The river snaked through the lush forest-garden, through the heart of Chattanooga. The Tennessee is true to its name, *Tanasi*—the place where the river bends, where the green water meets itself, where the pastoral terrain is full of peace. But do not be deceived. I stared at the colored bridge—once bright blue, now softened under the withering sun—arched over the Moccasin Bend water, its rye brown murk streaking through algae; sloshing the stained limestone pillars. On that day, the river seemed to cry, its elegiac tone rippling the water. I sensed the urgency of the river flow—as if it were carrying secrets far away—driven by undercurrents and a hapless wind, perhaps to assuage a certain kind of guilt when all creation groans.

The view of the second span in its Camelback truss design was particularly beautiful and ugly, indifferent and poignant. I held my breath to arrest the quiver in my hands, but the pigments at the end of my brush must have sensed I was still troubled. In the crux of the girders, their steel shadows failed to conceal all of it. Nor the rust—color of dried blood—could hide the ligature on the beams themselves from the sway and fray of rope that once hung there with a young Black man dangling on its end. Just like before. My canvas couldn't quite capture the right shade in those innocent flecks of red, the spilled blood. I heard the whispers in the latticework of the bridge: echoes from the crack of fifty some bullets that riddled his body, its thump after falling on the bridge walk when a bullet severed the hemp, the shattering of his skull from yet another five shots—point blank to the head, the raucous jeers from the crowd, the caws of crows drowning out his words of forgiveness for his murderers.

History cannot hide the bullet holes anymore than the bridge's wooden walkway could. Still life. And there's always a bigger problem. I could not find the depth of blackness in the corners of the beams, or in the swirls of water in the deepening umbra of the

96

waves, nor could I understand the grave color and texture of human hatred.

Author's Note: On March 19, 1906, Ed Johnson was hanged from the second span of the Walnut Street Bridge, and brutally mutilated for allegedly attacking and raping a white woman.

What Have I Done to His Handiwork?

Today *my heart* is a *vague trembling of stars*
and heavy with the universe
tucked into its folds. Who am I
to tread on the whispers
of God, He who fashioned
me from stardust? He has brought me
sunset in a cup, and I've spilled it.
I am the immense shadow of my tears.

With thanks to Federico García Lorca and Emily Dickinson

Water Cycle

When hope evaporates
from the ocean, and lofts
high into cold dry stratus,
a canopy of clouds hovering
over land like sadness
draping the heart, the sea
will also give up its prayers
to the sky.

There's always a gathering
of storms before the deluge
of pain, but a fresh rain also
from the same place comes
to wash it away—

at first in trickles and rivulets,
then the swelling into creeks,
the flowing as mighty rivers
from the watershed.

Eventually, all things return
to the sea, tears dissolving
into prayers.

Voices of Appalachia

An erasure poem from book titles in Appalachian Literature

Iron spirit of the mountains our southern home, the heart of earth. Night-death, day and time unforeseen, a red thread unquieting heaven, leaves the family a company of owls. Appalachia, remember the beautiful heroes, the good mountains, the divine time of man. Look homeward. Around us springs freedom.

Source material: 44 titles (from 30 authors) in Appalachian literature in order of appearance in the Wikipedia entry: http://en.wikipedia.org/wiki/Appalachia#Literature. Punctuation added.

Life in the Iron Mills; The Spirit of the Mountains; Our Southern Highlanders; Call Home to the Heart; The River of Earth; The Dollmaker; Night Comes to the Cumberlands; A Death in the Family; This Day and Time; Hannah Coulter; The Unforeseen Wilderness: An Essay on Kentucky's Red River Gorge; Taps for Private Tussie; The Thread That Runs So True; The Unquiet Earth; Storming Heaven; Fair and Tender Ladies, On Agate Hill, Clay's Quilt; A Parchment of Leaves; The Far Family, The Tall Woman; Bucolics; A Companion for Owls; Appalachian Studies; We Keep a Store; Borrowed Children; Don't You Remember?; Moon Women; The Big Beautiful; No Heroes; The Good Brother; Cold Mountain; Thirteen Moons; The Hangman's Beautiful Daughter; Gap Creek; The Brier Poems; Divine Right's Trip; Kinfolks; Serena, The Great Meadow, The Time of Man, Look Homeward, Angel; You Can't Go Home Again; The Sea Around Us; Silent Spring; Presidential Medal of Freedom; The Glass Castle

Kindling

Paper, crumbled
Brown leaves
Twigs thick as straw
Brittle stems
Spindle pine
Crisscrossed branches:
Pin oak, hickory, maple
Monument of wood
Standing quiet until
Silence breaks

Phosphor striking
Pungent, orange flame leaps
Devours paper as acid
Spreading on onion skin
Wood, submissive
Crackles over white noise
Smoke whistles
Plumes twist, split, spread
Scorched rafters
Firelight shines below
Ashen branches collapse
Under pull of lashing flame
Hollow cinders chime
Lumbered pieces fall
Glow red, streaks of dark
Transform to hot-star white

As wind blows through

Nature Is Loud but I Don't Hear Her

All the stars are singing
every color I can feel.

And I sing back my notes
of grief. I ponder each

tone, let the music
of the spheres subsume

the deep dark spaces
in my life. Does she understand?

Robert Frost asked the same
question when he chose

something like a star.
It remained taciturn, too.

I do not understand
the language of the stars

yet I should because
I am stardust.

Perhaps I should ask
the wind. It is blue

like the smile in your eyes.
But I cannot discern

the answer from the static
hiss of leaves.

I interrogate the ocean
sweeping wave after wave

of questions in its rhetoric
and I am left on the beach
        washed clean of answers.

So I look up, above the ocean,
past the wind, beyond the stars

and listen for that small
still voice.

Life Cycle

The life of mortals is like grass,
*   they flourish like a flower of the field;*
the wind blows over it and it is gone,
*   and its place remembers it no more.*
— Psalm 103:15-16

Flowers bloom with the rising
of the daffodil sun bursting
through the veil of morning

Throughout the day they raise
their sepals and petals in prayer
that canopy a lapis lazuli sky

Then kneel into dirt, well-rooted,
bow their once radiant heads
in somber purple of twilight

before resting in the sunset
of darkness, that black cosmos
of night, waiting, waiting

for resurrection, for the hope
of new day, with the promise
of fresh winds of change

Acknowledgments

101 Words [Star-filled Eyes]

2019 Chattanooga Writers' Guild Anthology [Aubade—contest finalist]

Anak Sastra [River Waking Mountains]

Artemis Journal [Some Say It's the Moonshine]

AUIS Literary Journal [I always carry my words and the sounds of my life]

Bloodroot: Literary Magazine of South Eastern Kentucky Community College [Working the Puzzle; Spring Cleaning by the Book with my Ex; My house; A Hundred Shades of Green Blaze the Trail; Nuggets of Coal]

Bradlaugh's Finger [Hoarding]

Braided Way [Life Cycle]

Conclave: Journal of Character [Bread & Butter Pickles]

Eye to the Telescope [undying—Best of the Net nominee, 2017]

I Thought I Heard A Cardinal Sing (Sheila-Na-Gig, ed. Kari Gunter-Seymour (Ohio Poet Laureate) [Speculators]

Impressions Literary Magazine [Black—winner of 2020 Impressions of Appalachian Creative Arts Contest in Poetry]

Inscape Literary Magazine [Condemned Property]

Litterateur: redefining world [The Path Taken; Wilderness]

Mildred Haun Review [The Crack in the Cookie Jar; Shiitake Mushrooms; Blood; Song of the Mountains (formerly Her Name

Is Tennessee); Engulfed; At a Writer's Retreat Near a Coalmining Town (hybrid); Nature is Loud but I Don't Hear Her]

Nadwah: Journal of Poetry in Translation [Collecting Stones with my Granddaughter]

Number One [Woodcarving]

On The Veranda Literary Journal [White Lightning]

Open Earth II-Ecopoetry (ed. Susann Moeller, Pudding Magazine Books, 2017) [Wild River; Resurrection]

Pine Mountain Sand & Gravel [Mountain Song; The Making of Steel; Death of a Mountain]

Poetry South [Breakfast at Midnight]

Pudding Magazine: The Journal of Applied Poetry [Chiseled in Stone]

Red Branch Review [The Walnut Street Bridge— winner 2017 Joy Margrave Award for Nonfiction (Tennessee Mountain Writers)]

Red Coyote Journal [Carrots]

The Rye Whiskey Review [High Definition; Lake Sign]

The Scriblerus Arts Journal [What Have I Done to His Handiwork]

Setu: A Bilingual and Peer-Reviewed Journal of Literature, Arts, and Culture [Water Cycle]

Skive Magazine [The Last Rose]

Songs of Eretz Poetry Review [Water Ritual; Slickrock Wilderness; Falling/Leaves; Ode to Sunflowers]

Static Poetry II (ed. Chris Bartholomew, Static Movement Publishing, 2011) [Everything Is Regional]

The Syzygy Poetry Journal [The Scattering of Stars]

Town Creek Poetry [Kindling]

Transformative Power of Art Journal [Antietam National Battlefield Museum: A Poem]

Voices on the Wind: Mountain Voices [Carolina Special]

Wood Cat Review [Dead Logs in the Stream]

Artemis Journal [Some Say It's the Moonshine; Edge Effect]

Author's Bio

John C. Mannone has poems in *North Dakota Quarterly, Pine Mountain Sand & Gravel, Artemis Journal, Red Branch Review, Poetry South, Baltimore Review, Pedestal, New England Journal of Medicine,* and many others. He won the Impressions of Appalachia Creative Arts Contest in poetry (2020), the Joy Margrave Award for creative nonfiction (2015 and 2017), and the Carol Oen Memorial Fiction Prize (2020). He was awarded a Jean Ritchie Fellowship (2017) in Appalachian literature and served as the celebrity judge for the National Federation of State Poetry Societies (2018). He is the author of three chapbooks and several full-length collections, *Disabled Monsters* (2015) and *Flux Lines* (2022) with Linnet's Wings Press and *Sacred Flute* forthcoming (2024) from Iris Press. He edits poetry for *Abyss & Apex* and other journals. He is a professor of physics and chemistry, and invited professor of creative writing in poetry, at Alice Lloyd College in southeastern Kentucky.

http://jcmannone.wordpress.com
https://www.facebook.com/jcmannone

Middle Creek Publishing & Audio

MIDDLE CREEK PUBLISHING believes that responding to the world through art & literature — and sharing that response — is a vital part of being an artist.

MIDDLE CREEK PUBLISHING is a company seeking to make the world a better place through both the means and ends of publishing. We are publishers of quality literature in any genre from authors and artists, both seasoned and as-yet undervalued, with a great interest in works which may be considered to be, illuminate or embody any aspect of contemplative Human Ecology, defined as the relationship between humans and their natural, social, and built environments.

MIDDLE CREEK's particular interest in Human Ecology, is meant to clarify an aspect of the quality in the works we will consider for publication, and is meant as a guide to those considering submitting work to us. Our interest is in publishing works illuminating the Human experience through words, story or other content that connects us to each other, our environment, our history, and our potential deeply and more consciously.

Made in the USA
Monee, IL
17 October 2023

44773318R10070